Piece of Mind

Cass Hempel

BookLeaf Publishing

India | USA | UK

Presentation by *BookLeaf Publishing*

Web: www.bookleafpub.com

E-mail: info@bookleafpub.com

ISBN: 9789358315929
First edition 2023

DEDICATION

This is dedicated to everyone in my life that only ever wanted me to succeed.

Especially my Momma, who always believed in me.

ACKNOWLEDGEMENT

Thank you to the internet algorithm, they know exactly what I need before I knew I needed it!

Wake-up

1

I no longer want to sleep, and hide away from
you.
Emerging from the haze, I called my everyday
life.
Waking up and living now, trying out new
things.
Rediscovering passions, I thought lost long ago.
Showing the side I smothered in vice, fearing the
unknown.
Here I am, world!
I might not be ready, but I'm willing to give it a
try.

Bedtime

As we lay in silence
I hear your thoughts so loud
I just want to feel peace
While you work towards being proud
I wonder how much longer
We continue our charade
How much more time till my heart explodes
Like it has enveloped a grenade
I just want transparency
Like we had when this all started
Not this game of half truths
Your intentions left uncharted

Gratitude

Grateful for recovery
Staying sober every day
And having the ability
To live life in a new way

Grateful for the fellowship
The people by my side
They refuse to be pushed away
No matter how hard I've tried

Grateful for the life
I now look forward to living
And wanting to stop the take
And do more of the giving

Grateful for new passions
And old ones to be reclaimed
And wearing my past on my sleeve
No longer feeling ashamed

Grateful for the tools
And how I've learned to cope
With stress of daily life
And always having hope

Grateful for the friends
I've made along the way
And knowing I can do this forever
If I only think about today

Mindless

Itchy feet and wandering dreams
Nothing is ever as it seems
Sometimes I just want to get away
Where no one can hear my silent screams

Bad days come and good days go
These are all things I know
Parts of our stories and our lives
Put there to help us grow

Sometimes I laugh and then I'll cry
Getting lost in the reasons why
But as long I want to keep on learning
I've got to be willing to try

Mindset

Feeling light and feeling free
Basking in the wonder that is me
Not a cloud in the sky nor in sight
Just loving the mood I'm in tonight

Great fellowship and friends around
Trying new places right here in town
Giving back what I took from the start
Is the only thing that heals my heart

Now nestled so cozy in bed
Keeping happy thoughts in my head
While my whole world crashes down
At least I'll still have them around

Ignoring temptation in that top drawer
Knowing what the universe has in store
The laws of vibration will work their ways
And have always shown me better days

If I keep doing good and really believe
There's no limit to what I'll achieve
I won't be stopped or contained
By those who seem to live to complain

I'll shatter my goals and live my dreams
And be exactly who I seem
And anyone who won't keep up
Will simply be left behind in the dust

Self love

I saw myself in the mirror today
And I think I liked what I'd seen
Someone who tries to love and be loved
Someone who's sober and clean

I saw a girl once so lost in the mess
Now finding her way to peace
Serenity is the name of the game
And the terrors have seemed to ceased

A reflection I saw staring back at me
Of someone I thought long gone
A face of a lady I recognized
And of whom I've grown quite fond

Someone I saw today staring back at me
Making the moves I made
I realized it only takes one slip
And into the darkness, she'll fade.

A.M.

It's 3 a.m. and you're nowhere to be found
By now it's the norm and I'm used to the sound
Of the silent house and a broken heart
And I sit here and wonder what is my part
I've allowed this to go on for far too long
While you chase a siren's song
In the dead of night you steal away
And I grow tired of this game you play
I want to think you love me the best you can
When I know you could be a better man
This whole experience has me jaded
Every night I wonder about this life I traded
Once so free and learning to trust
Gave it all up for a moment of lust
Seeing your secrets made me have my own
We play games as if we're not grown
Whatever you're doing, I took it too far
And the ending is gonna leave a helluva scar

Spiritual Fitness

Lifted spirits
Heightened hearts
Finding light
Within the dark

Knowing the value
Assigning my worth
Making the most
Of my time on earth

Working with others
Esteemable acts
Walking with grace
Speaking with tact

Reflecting daily
On the path I have chosen
Where everything moves on
Nothing left frozen

This is how my spirit
Gets its exercise
Or else I prepare
For spiritual demise

Over

I feel the hate resonate and I don't know what to
do
I want to be so angry but you were only being
you
My whole life turned upside down in the matter
of a minute
Everyone with their suggestions, but they aren't
living in it
Now all I want to do is cry about how life ain't
fair
I need someone to turn to for comfort, but
surprise! You're not there
Thank heavens for the program in which I'm
involved
Otherwise I'd be solving these problems with
drugs and alcohol
I can't believe I let you in, to break my heart
again
So many petty texts I've written, but just can't
seem to send
The worst part of it is I still think we could make
this work
But I don't think you'll ever change and you'll
always be a jerk

Hopefulness

The world seems calm
The air feels so clean
Possibilities are endless
And the mood is serene

This is the weather
After the storm
Where some will fall
And others perform

This is the moment
To swim or sink
Process and proceed
Instead of overthink

When the world ends
A beginning arises
Full of hope
And pleasant surprises

Shiny

The way he put his lips on mine
And puts his hands all on my body
Gives me feelings I forgot I had
Ones that turn me naughty

A single look he gives
Makes my body quiver
I can't wait to show him
That I'm really more of a giver

A forbidden fruit the flavor
I want to taste so bad
I can not stay away for long
Now that a bite, I've had

Wind in my hair and past behind
Speeding through the doubt
Can not wait to have my chance
And show what love's about

Birthday

Celebrated my birthday today
Did not go as planned
Wandering the lonely roads
Far across the land

Wishing I was with you
And that you were still around
Feeling lost and hopeless
And never being found

All in all it turned out
To be a decent day
But that didn't matter because
Without you, I'm just not okay

Wishing I had never looked
And found your little stash
Because everything I'm doing now
Is just to pad my crash

I wish you'd just say sorry
Pretend that you felt bad
Understand my heartbreak
And why you make me sad

I thought we'd be together
On the day of my birth
But I need to keep my value
And understand what I am worth

A new day

The moon sets once again
And the sun starts shining
I'm doing everything I can
To stop all my whining

Distractions all around me
So I don't overthink anymore
Trying to see the brighter side
And know what I'm doing this for

Surround myself with compassion
And give a little grace
And know I'm where I need to be
Since life is not a race

Found love where I thought was lost
And passions I'd forgotten
Pruning the tree of my circle of friends
And tossing all who are rotten

A new life waits for me
Without you by my side
And I lament all the time
And wasted tears I cried

It's time to restart and refocus
Take it minute by minute they say
I know this will hurt again
But it doesn't have to today

Changes

A long way I have come
From who I used to be
Living a life I wouldn't recognize
Never have I felt so free

Sometimes I think back
To the person I was
Using whomever I could
To catch my next buzz

Now I feel things
Whether good or bad
I've come to love the happy days
But man, I hate being sad

I care about those around me
Even people I don't know
I give shit how they are feeling
And I hope to watch them grow

I'm taking on the wretched steps
One day at a time
Trying out all the A's
Living in my prime

Some have watched me flourish
Others saw me fall
All I know is they will answer
Everytime I call

My family wants me around
Well, most anyways
My daughter and the stepmother
Still don't have much to say

I've caused a lot of pain
In the process of addiction
And everyday I wanna wake up
And find out it's all a work of fiction

But this is my reality
I do all to excess
An allergy of my body
Causes my brain to obsess

I do the work
And lay the ground
For the new life
I have found

Hasten

Life caught up to me
And I fell behind
But with a new vigor
I will continue on
It might be half-hearted
It might not be my best
But I will prevail
And I know I can do this
Without falling again
This will be my greatest feat

Jamming

In my truck I drive alone
Radio up and windows down
Forget the pain
And turn up the song

I love the feeling
Loudly singing
Loudly and off key
Sends my heart reeling

I can avoid my stress
And ignore the mess
Flying high alone
And leaving the rest

Wind Therapy

I went over 100 today
Felt the wind on my face
Might've been through a helmet
But I think I've found my place

Felt so free and alive
Can't wait to ride again
Maybe do it just for fun
Maybe learn to win

I feel the wheels on the ground
And the horsepower in my heart
The miles in my veins
I'm fresh but it's a start

Helmet now imperative
In my daily routine
I feel safe and free
And mostly I feel serene

Finish Line

I've written the words
We've traveled my world
Through the trials and tribulations
Truths have definitely unfurled

I am still clean and sober
Despite my love turning me over
Finding drugs in my house
And not even covert

I've found love from the rooms
And life will soon improve
Setting solid boundaries
And making the right moves

Trying out new things
Taking shit for as it seems
Learning about myself
And finding out my team